CHALAM

Sudha
(*Nectar*)

Sudha
(Nectar)

CHALAM

MOTILAL BANARSIDASS/UNESCO

First Edition : Delhi 1990

MOTILAL BANARSIDASS
Bungalow Road, Jawahar Nagar, Delhi-110 007

Branches:
Chowk, Varanasi 221 001
Ashok Rajpath, Patna 800 004
24 Race Course Road, Bangalore 560 001
120 Royapettah High Road, Mylapore, Madras 600 004

UNESCO COLLECTION OF REPRESENTATIVE WORKS
INDIAN SERIES
This book, translated from the Telugu, has been accepted in the translation collection of the United Nations Educational, Scientific and Cultural Organization (UNESCO).

Translated from the Telugu by J.S.R.L. Narayana Moorty, Elliot Roberts, Sowris Pramoda, and Julie Wellings.

ISBN: 81-208-0614-x

PRINTED IN INDIA
BY JAINENDRA PRAKASH JAIN AT SHRI JAINENDRA PRESS, A-45 NARAINA INDUSTRIAL AREA, PHASE I, NEW DELHI 110028 AND PUBLISHED BY NARENDRA PRAKASH JAIN FOR MOTILAL BANARSIDASS, DELHI 110007.

Dedicated to
Īśwara
who is
incarnated
in the heart of
Sowris

CONTENTS

INTRODUCTION

'Chalam' (Gudipati Venkatachalam) was born to Brahmin parents in the city of Madras in 1894; he died in May, 1979, in Tiruvannamalai, in the Indian state of Tamil Nadu. As his father was unemployed and without income, and as his maternal grandfather did not have sons of his own to perform his funeral and memorial rites, the latter adopted Chalam with the hope that he would perform them when he died. Thus, Chalam's childhood was spent in a family consisting of himself, his sisters, his parents, and his maternal grandparents.

Although the young Chalam lived amidst wealth and luxury thanks to his grandfather's status as government official, his boyhood was a troubled one. He suffered constant physical abuse from his father; much of it related to his father's attempts to educate his son. This abuse once and for all set Chalam against the harsh, parental authority traditional to India and, later, against the then current English-style educational system in India. He thought children should be treated as friends. Rejecting authority based on physical punishment, Chalam believed parents should use rational persuasion with their children. The educational system, he later complained, suppressed and thwarted the spirit of young boys and girls and made them merely socially respectable instead of enabling them to be open to and enjoy the beauties of life.

Chalam was raised a devout Hindu. He performed various Hindu religious rituals, worshipped God daily, read the scriptures and, at his home, listened to Hindu scholars expound upon these scriptures. To his young mind, the fates some of the scriptural characters suffered seemed unfair; and when he questioned his mother, who read the texts to him, he was not satisfied with her answers.

Although he vowed he wouldn't marry, while still young he made friends with several girls and played with them, an uncommon practice for the youth of this time. However, as he was still young and couldn't dare leave home and live on his own, he had to yield to the pressure of his elders and marry. After his marriage in 1910 at the age of 16, however, he began to practice his unorthodox ideals in his home. He encouraged his young wife to rebel against the authority of her in-laws, to get an education by going to school or by being coached at home, and later to work as an insurance agent.

At the age of 17 Chalam entered college at Kakinada (Pithapuram Raja's College) and came under the influence of Raghupati Venkataratnam Naidu, the then principal of the college and a well-known intellectual leader of Brahmo Samaj. Brahmo Samaj, a socio-religious movement, was founded in India in 1828 by Raja Ram Mohan Roy. Under the influence of Christianity and the West, it denounced image worship, advocated a benevolent, monotheistic God, and espoused social reform aimed at eradicating divisions of caste, race, sex, and religion, including liberation of women and remarriage of widows. It avowed a life of love, truthfulness, morality, and devotion to and striving for God.

In Chalam's youth, Brahmo Samaj swept through Andhra (then part of Madras State) and the rest of India. Chalam fell under its influence, and for a number of years espoused its ideals. Its leaders—like Ram Mohan Roy and Kandukuri Veeresalingam Pantulu—had a significant effect upon his thinking. He eschewed image worship and rituals. While at college he was boycotted by his fellow students for having dined with a student from a non-Brahmin caste, and, as a result, he began questioning the validity of the Hindu caste system. When one of his younger sisters was to be married against her will to a young man Chalam and others considered unworthy, he tried to apply Brahmo Samaj's views on women's liberation to her situation. First, he tried to help her out of the marriage; later, when this failed, out of her being forced into the nuptial bed. However, when his sister came out of the nuptial room the next morning, she no longer complained about her marriage. Later, she accused Chalam of trying to break up her marriage. His failure taught him the cost of advocating reform—for his efforts he could expect rebuff and lack of appreciation.

Some years later Chalam alienated himself from the official Brahmo Samaj movement when he could no longer tolerate what he saw as hypocrisy concerning caste and marriage among its followers. On the one hand, its leaders were denouncing caste; but, on the other, one of them had joined the caste-oriented Justice Party. The leaders would talk of widow marriages, yet they would force unwed mothers into marriages against their will just to save their respectability.

In 1930, when Chalam's first-born child died at the age of 14 of an incurable illness after suffering for seven years, Chalam's faith in God was shaken, and he became for some years a skeptic and an atheist. Because his mind was never closed, he looked for something else to give meaning to his life. For a long time to come, Chalam would find such meaning in relationships with women, in sex, romance, and love. Despite his marriage and to the utter dismay of his wife, he obsessively sought an idealized woman in extramarital relationships. Once, later in his life, he thought he had found such a woman; however, she turned against him because she could not keep him exclusively to herself. That cured Chalam of his obsession with the "woman of his dreams."

The religious piety of Chalam's childhood later turned into a spiritual quest for some higher meaning in life which would somehow reconcile him to the world and to existence itself. As he wrote in his *Autobiography:*

> There has always been a battle between my life and myself. Ever since I was conscious, I had the conviction that this world must be a playground for every living being, a playground devoid of any fear, pain or suffering. But as I looked more and more, it appeared not as a playground but as a ground of battles and wounds, a suffering-ground of sick people who are beaten down every day, every minute. This is why my struggle is not only with my own pain, but with all the pain in the world, with all darkness.[1]

He sought this higher meaning through art, through his appreciation of nature, through romantic love, and, in the latter part of his life, through spiritual practices under the guidance of his daughter, Sowris. Among his five children, Sowris was the one who remained closest to Chalam. From early childhood she showed spiritual proclivities and was educated mostly by her father's writings, as she did not have much of a formal education.

Indian society's brutal oppression and persecution of women offended the young Chalam deeply. He attacked his society for its hypocrisy towards and oppression of women, for its snobbery and love of respectability. He wrote:

> Women should have equal rights with men in all matters including sex. For ages woman has been a slave to man. The society of men has oppressed women. It could not imagine that she is a person, that she has individuality, and that she too has likes and dislikes, interests and love of freedom. Man has regarded woman as a mechanical doll which procreated children and cooked for him. This is unfair. Women too must have the freedom which men have. Until then her individuality does not become perfected.[2]

Chalam believed that women should have freedom and equality with men, even if it meant the collapse of society and anarchy. As long as women were not treated as human, he believed, society was structured on a false foundation. At the same time, Chalam is critical of modern women who have only achieved a superficial freedom:

> The modern woman who is escaping the authority and control of the husband is becoming a slave to fashion and social respectability. A housewife who could defy society standing in the shadow of her husband is now a slave to thousands in the name of fashion, job, and respectability. For the modern woman all the women around her have become mothers-in-law.[3]

During his middle years (1920-1950), Chalam worked as a school teacher and a deputy inspector of schools in the Education Department of the then Madras government. He never fully adjusted to this work, because of his disapproval of the type of education that was given in the schools and because of his difficulty in conforming to the dictates of authority.

In 1936, Chalam visited Sri Ramana Maharshi, an Indian mystic who taught a form of Vedānta philosophy. While visiting at Tiruvannamalai, Chalam was deeply impressed by Sri Ramana's spiritual personality. Sowris accompanied her father on some of these visits. In 1950, the year of Sri Ramana Maharshi's death, Chalam retired with his family to Tiruvannamalai and remained there until his own death.

At Tiruvannamalai, Chalam and Sowris, after having practiced Yoga for some time, took up the form of meditation taught by Sri Ramana Maharshi. In this meditation, as each thought or emotion arises, one inquires of oneself, "Who am I?" Sowris, who had been an undeclared pupil of Ramana Maharshi, went into trances during these meditations and was supposed to have advanced so high spiritually that she, her father, and the people around her believed that God spoke through her. Although she was a talented writer, Sowris at this time gave up her writing in favor of her spiritual practice. Inspired, she spoke to Chalam and answered his spiritual doubts, got rid of his chronic migraine headaches by putting him through a regimen of Yoga practices, and collaborated with him on several of his spiritual and poetical writings. Chalam wrote of himself at this stage of his life:

> Something which never happened in human history in any age to any man, prophet or yogi, is happening in our family.

> God, besides living with us in our family and making us strive for spiritual experience, is sharing our daily joys and sorrows. He is explaining to us, mixing his teaching with our day-to-day activity, how his creation goes on, why he does not remove all these sufferings, how there happens to be a harmony in him between infinite love and interminable cruelty, how he is bound in every minute and every atom, and how there is justice in Karma. He is making us practice selfless action and great Yoga, enabling us to move our feet, correcting our mistakes, scolding us, cajoling us, and shedding light on us increasingly. When such a thing is happening, how can I keep quiet?[4]

Prior to this time, Chalam's life had been one of constant struggle. His writings centered around problems of women and his own spiritual investigations. Because of his writings and his life-style, he faced opposition from the society around him. People would not rent him apartments in towns; so he sometimes had to live outside of towns in thatched huts among untouchables. He would shelter women who ran away from troubled homes, women who had unwanted pregnancies, and women looking for work. He had to answer to their husbands, parents, and relatives in person and, at times, in courts of law.

Economically, he was never well-off, as he relinquished his rights to his inheritance, being disgusted with the greed of his parents who, he felt, valued property more than their children. His own income was always modest. From his writings he had practically no income: although publishers eagerly solicited his work, most of them never paid him any royalties after publication.

Chalam possessed a gentle, friendly and rather shy disposition. He loved jokes and good humor, appreciated nature, delighted in conversations with friends, and enjoyed relationships with women. More than anything else, he loved truth and living according to what he believed to be the truth. He disliked arguments and quarrels, but, once he got involved in a dispute, he would rather forego his friendship than try to please someone by telling him pleasant falsehoods.

Chalam's writings mirror his life. Just as he tried to live what he preached, so his writings reflected what he was living.

> I am not just a writer. My writing is a product of my life. I am a preacher and teacher by birth. The enthusiasm that I should by some means or other open men's eyes

> overwhelms me. Personally I am neutral. I don't preach anyone anything. I can't even speak when I am asked to. But when I take a pen, words go out of my control. The inspiration that I should tell the truth I know one way or the other overtakes me . . . . The scoldings in my books alienated many decent people from me and threatened even those who loved me as a human being.[5]

Chalam's writing career began at age 16 with an unfinished translation of a novel by Henry Wood. He started writing for personsal reasons—to get back at a stronger cousin who had beaten him. To avenge himself, he gave the villain in the novel his cousin's name. In his 69 years as a writer, he produced some 70 published works. He worked in many different forms: essays, novels, plays, short stories, letters, translations, autobiography, and poetry. His writings can be divided into two periods which correspond to the two major periods in his life—pre-Ramaṇāśramaṁ, those works written before he retired to Tiruvannamalai, and post-Ramaṇāśramaṁ (c. 1950 and after).

Except for an essay called "Man and Woman" written in English in 1926, all Chalam's writings are primarily in Telugu, one of the four major Dravidian languages spoken in the South of India. Chalam never cared very much for rules of language or of poetry when he wrote. He would not hesitate to use an occasional English word or expression, sometimes without even transliterating it into the Telugu script. He first wrote a few essays in classical Telugu—the language of the traditionally-accepted literary style—, but soon abandoned it in favor of a more accessible colloquial Telugu. He never consciously cultivated a style. He says of his style and writing:

> The man who came to visit me said, "let alone your opinions, your style is unique." I don't insist that you should agree with my opinions, but I get indignant if people separate my style from them. If anyone asks what the word 'style' means, it implies that my opinions are all right, but he doesn't have the courage to accept them. They think that style is something you practice like a trick, that if they can discover that secret, they too can write that way. How could I convey to them that I don't know what style is, that they can find that from the scholars, that I didn't even know that I could write until this woman problem came and boiled the blood in my heart, until I got furious against society's persecution of women without understanding them, and

> that even now I can't write about anything else? By practicing you can improve your style, but the emotion has to come effortlessly from the heart. By picking and arranging words, we can amaze others, but we cannot provoke their hearts. For blood to spill from one's pen, one must suffer and be crushed under the wheels of life's chariot. My writing is not letters nor scholarship. Years of silent suffering, search in darkness, the secret tragedy in the hearts of creatures like me, the suppressed anger of the helpless and the weak, the wailings of the 'lowly characters' which cannot be told to anyone—this is my style.[6]

Chalam's writings are, as the above indicates, highly emotional. While their expression is in clear, direct prose, a great deal of poetry exists in his writing, although except in *Sudha* and *Chalam Gītālu* (*Chalam's Songs,* 1954) he did not choose to express himself in poetical form. In his prose, Chalam enjoys scolding his readers; in the middle of telling a story, he will, in his own voice, present tirades against society.

Another outstanding quality of his fiction is the compelling nature of his storytelling, perhaps gained from his study of the works of de Maupassant. Although his central characters—almost exclusively women—do and say the most unconventional and sometimes outrageous things openly and courageously, Chalam makes us feel that these are what *we* have been thinking all the time and what *we* wanted to say or do ourselves, but dared not. Although he lectures his readers in his own voice in the midst of his narratives, he does so in a way which does not alienate his readers. Stylistically and thematically, his critiques of society's customs, traditions, and moral codes remind us of Bernard Shaw and Henrik Ibsen.

Chalam's works show the influence of many writers: Rabindranath Tagore, Count Maeterlinck, Havelock Ellis, Guy de Maupassant, and Bertrand Russell—all of whom Chalam read either in school or on his own. His writings reflect Tagore's appreciation of nature and its beauty, his devotion to God through art, de Maupassant's art of storytelling, Bertrand Russell's ideas concerning marriage and morals, and his free thinking in general, Havelock Ellis' ideas concerning relationships between men and women, and Maeterlinck's questioning concerning God and the mystery of life. According to Achanta Janakiram,

> Chalam proved (in his plays) what needed change could be brought about in our language and in our ideas through the

contact with the wealth of Western literature.[7]

Chalam's writings have been compared to those of a 17th Century Telugu writer, Vēmana, primarily in that they both offered a critique of their society, their writings were didactic, and both were interested in the spiritual uplift of the individual. Sri Sri, the foremost of the Telugu modern progressive poets, says of Chalam:

> Chalam propounds the doctrine of free life in his writings. He asserts that man must break through layers of artificial civilization and live very naturally like animals and birds. He says the same thing concerning women and even concerning the rearing of children.[8]

Chief among Chalam's essays are *Strī* (*Woman*, 1924), *Biḍḍala Śikṣaṇa* (*Training of Children*, 1924), *Musings* (1944), *Prēma Lēkhalu* (*Love Letters*, 1944), *Ānandaṁ* (*Joy*, 1944), *Viṣādaṁ* (*Sorrow*, 1944), and *Chalam Uttarālu* (*Chalam's Letters*, 1945). In these and other essays, Chalam expresses his view that Hindu culture has lost its vitality because of its hypocrisy. While superficially imitating Western culture—its industrialism, socialism, and modern warfare—Hindus speak of God's will, karma, *māyā*, and so on, without practicing these religious precepts. Chalam's hope is that his criticism will someday bring about a change:

> There is some wisdom in individuals and societies. Man has the ability to protect himself no matter how many people pull him in whatever direction. No matter how much people tell him, no matter how much his own mind sways, at the end he depends on his own inner wisdom. The same with society. It needs its customs of its own time whether they be good or bad. They have been tested by age and found wholesome. Time tested and sustained them. The reforms you and I teach today may be very true and necessary; but thousands like us are shouting in society's ear, gathering around her. If it sways with whatever everyone says, it will be subject to the same fate as a sick man who drinks every medicine that is sold in the market. That is why, no matter who extols or scolds her, society stands steady and thinks like a buffalo being beaten. One of those times it moves . . . what we tell her it takes in gradually and thinks somewhere inside. Meanwhile it swats with its tail noisy bees like us who make too much noise.
>
> But it moves-one of those times, when it feels like. Unless we agitate, it won't move . . . . What is true, what is healthy for herself, it takes time to decide. Meanwhile those

> who shout become fewer. A few selfish people, cheats, some who don't have patience and perseverance, one or two of them remain. Many will die before they attain the embrace of the maiden called society.[9]

According to Bucchi Babu, Chalam did indeed move society through his agitation:

> Chalam's writings have caused a new outlook in the Andhra public. The moral outlook of men and women has broadened. Chalam thus is a great social reformer who achieved reform through his writings. Veeresalingam brought about a change in the gross world, in the social system. But the change that Chalam has brought about is in the human heart.[10]

Chalam believed that even if political systems and social conditions were changed, we could not save mankind, for man's suffering would not cease. All over the universe there is suffering, physical and mental, manifest and unmanifest: a result of the omnipresent struggle, the yearning to reach something, the dissatisfaction with one's own condition. Man's suffering will not cease, because there is a higher quest in him that seeking political and social changes simply will not satisfy. Real change must come from within. For Chalam, the transformation that can occur within an individual is more valuable than any change that occurs in society.

To get to know the peace in oneself, one must not seek outer pleasures; through living truthfully and virtuously, one reaches peace. For Chalam, there is no universal moral code. Thinking that one's opinion alone is right and that there is a universal moral code is the cause of untold misery in mankind. Spirituality consists in opening one's eyes to the beauty and joy in the universe.

Within this ethos, education and art become very important for Chalam. Education should help a child enjoy life and its beauty; it should enable the child to escape life's vicissitudes and avoid a self-centeredness which can come in the way of others' freedom. Art, because it creates beauty far greater than the beauty we can perceive with our physical senses, enhances and cultivates our spirituality. For Chalam, the artist who creates and the viewer who enjoys form a cultural aristocracy.

Some of Chalam's important novels are: *Śaśirēkha* (1921), *Daivamiccina Bhārya* (*God-Given Wife*, 1923), *Maidānaṁ* (*Open Space*, 1927), *Vivāhaṁ* (*Marriage*, 1928), *Aruṇa* (1935), *Brāhmaṇīkaṁ* (*Brahminness*, 1937), *Amīnā* (1940), *Haṁpī Kanyalu* (*Hampi Damsels*, 1944), and *Jīvitādarśam* (*Ideal of Life*, 1958). Several of his plays are also well-known: *Sāvitri* (1924), *Hariścandra* (1924), *Jayadeva* (1935), *Mṛtyuvu* (Death, 1935), and *Purūrava* (1947).

All the novels and plays, with one exception, are centered around women and their problems of sex, romance, and oppression by the moral codes and hypocrisies of society. Chalam's women follow their "heart," even if it means being whimsical, loving more than one man at the same time, and causing jealousy. His women are outspoken, and Chalam sympathizes with them, being even more outspoken in his scoldings of society than his heroines. They make love in open places, on river banks, in parks; Chalam describes their loves, their sacrifices, their jokes, their sorrows, and their tragedies with passion. They have no respect for rules of marriage and respectability. They rebel both openly and secretly against their husbands, their elders, and society.

Maidānaṁ is a typical work of this kind. In this novel, Rājēswari elopes from her Hindu lawyer-husband's home with a Moslem youth, Amīr, but also falls in love with another youth, Mīrā. She takes both as lovers, and soon becomes pregnant. An outcaste because of her life-style, she gives birth to a child alone, while Amīr, in a fit of jealousy, kills his rival suitor, Mīrā. During the investigation of the murder, Rājeswari is imprisoned for her improprieties. From her cell she writes a letter in which she justifies her actions and accuses society for her plight. Her letter is the conclusion of the novel. It was just such qualities as these in *Maidānaṁ*—attacks on traditional morality and explicit descriptions of sex—that made it almost impossible for the young to read Chalam's early works openly.

Several of Chalam's plays contain plots and characters taken from history and traditional Hindu mythology, but he recasts them according to his own views. Generally, his plots would be traditional, but the characters, particularly women, say and do things as Chalam's women usually do. For instance, Hariścandra in the play by his name (taken from the Hindu work of mythology, *Mārkaṇḍeya Purāṇa*), traditionally seen as a heroic figure who lost his kingdom and son because of his unwillingness to lie, is depicted by Chalam as a coward who sold his own wife and children to keep his moral code of truthful speaking. The character Sāvitri, in the play by her name (taken from a story in the *Mahābhārata)*, traditionally treated as a character who brought her husband back from the god of Death by standing up to his tests, is depicted as a woman who wins back her dead husband by offering her own body as an object of sexual enjoyment. In the play *Mṛtyuvu (Death)*, Chalam himself appears as one of the characters facing God and his final judgement after death.

Chalam's post-Ramaṇāśramaṁ writings (from around 1950) tend to be more poetic and spiritual and less issue-centered than his earlier writings. They were done under the influence of Sri Ramana Maharshi's teachings and under the supervision and guidance of "God", whom Chalam believed to be speaking through Sowris. As he said in *Musings*, his life had been transformed:

> Today my outlook has changed completely. The things that I blindly believed when I was young and later discarded as being far from truth are becoming evident today.
>
> I feel as if my life is beginning now. A ripping energy is coming out of me. My headaches are gone. Because of intense practice I get spells of laziness in the afternoon. That's all. I feel as if all my life is ahead of me.
>
> All my life I have been seeking beauty. I have realized it now to my utter satisfaction.[11]

Chalam translated some of Tagore's works and wrote his own introductions to them (e.g.,*Gītānjali*, 1958, *Phala Sēkaraṇa-Fruit Gathering*, 1967, and *Vanamāli-Gardner*, 1970). He translated and rewrote the stories of the Gospels, wrote a novel called *Mārtā* and a biography of Jesus. He also translated the *Bhagavad Gītā* (1966) and wrote his autobiography (1973).

Sudha (Nectar), written in 1961, culminates his spiritual quest, representing his personal, mystical experiences of the time. *Sudha*, one of his two works of poetry, is still in the mainstream of his writings, reflecting both his spiritual endeavors and his emphasis on love as one of the means of spiritual liberation. While Chalam of the earlier writings rebels against society and its moral codes, asking questions concerning the meaning of existence, Chalam in *Sudha* has answers to these questions. Still a non-conformist, he has transcended the social criticism of the earlier times.

Like all Chalam's writings, the style of *Sudha* is direct and poignant. One finds his usual railing against hypocrisy and false seekers of truth. Although contemporary Telugu poetry is bound by rules of grammar, meter, imagery, and rhyme, *Sudha* does not observe any such rules. In this respect, Chalam's poetry is akin to the style of progressive contemporary Telugu poets like Sri Sri and Arudra. Although *Sudha* does not use conventional meter, imagery, and rhyme, it has a heavy, powerful and recitable quality to it. This is achieved by an extensive use of Sanskrit vocabulary (about 90% of the words are Sanskrit). A typical poem starts with a series of highly Sanskritic compound words (technically called *samāsas*) and abruptly drops down toward the end of the poem into a few, light Telugu words, giving a sense of relief from the heaviness of the poem. This is part of the stylistic uniqueness of *Sudha*.

Consisting of 108 poems, *Sudha* chronicles Chalam's spiritual enlightenment. It begins with his physical awakening, as the rising sun illuminates the sacred mountain of Aruṇācala; it ends with his spiritual awakening, as the universal divine light infuses his soul. *Sudha* reveals Chalam's later view that the mind is what prevents us from knowing the questions it raises. When the mind is quiet, the answers become evident. Chalam expresses the contrast between his earlier quest and his experiences narrated in *Sudha* as follows:

> ...Before I came to Aruṇācala my philosophy was "No matter how much we try, we cannot know truth. At best we can approximate it." But today I know for certain that there is nothing there to know. Nothing. The more we try to know, the farther we are removed from truth. Because there *is* really nothing. When we know that there *is* really nothing, that means we know everything. But that 'nothing' is not a mere nothingness. It is a nothing which is illuminated by bliss. Yet it is neither bliss nor light. It is a nothing which encompasses and transcends them.[12]

Monterey,
California
July 25, 1987.

J.S.R.L. Narayana Moorty
Elliot Roberts

SUDHA
(Nectar)

I

Awake!

The flame flowers
which brightened
the dark hair of night
have fallen
on the bed of light
and faded away.

The dark sky is streaked
with the imprints
of the sharp rays
of the sun's fingernails.

On the Eastern flank of Aruṇācala
a vermilion worship[1]
is taking place.

Awake!

II

The Lord of night,[2]
yearning for a last glance from you,
waits at the window
with cupped hands.[3]

The cool sunshine,
arriving at the bedside,
is inviting your mind,
sunk in sleep,
to the celebration
of a new day.

The cool mountain breeze,
attracted by the fragrance of Kētaki,[4]
tangled in the mysterious,
dark recesses of your hair,
is begging
to be released.

Open your eyes!

III

Come with me to Aruṇācala!

The shadow of the banyan,
the flow of the stream,
a song on your lips,
and you
by my side.

Drunk with the honey from newly blossomed flowers,
the sunbirds, singing with intoxication;

The waves of wind touching softly
with the smoothness of tender Rāvi[5] leaves;

The temple bells ringing in the distance;

The shadows of clouds encircling the peak;

The fragrance of mountain grass and wild jasmine.

From the spheres of the sky
the plaintive call of the eagle;
the longing cry of the dove
for her mate.

IV

The Lord of the stars,[6]
who sported with Rōhiṇī[7]
in the mansions of the sky,
is preparing for a dip
in the Western ocean
alone.

Does Rōhiṇī know
she will be separated from him tonight?

V

The koel is cooing,
The wind is swinging
on the locks of your curly hair.
The sunshine
is gliding from your cheeks
onto your breasts!

VI

Look!

The goddess of the woods has decorated herself
for your arrival.
From the branch over your head
the *ponna*[8] flowers peep at you,
wondering who you are.

At the touch of your feet the meadow,
with irrepressible joy,
breaks out
in white flower-laughter.
The water of the stream
leaps from the rocks
to reach your face.

Dattura[9] worships the sun
with the glistening
of her white flowers.

VII

Just the other day, I lay in my bed
not quite awake.
The dawn looked startled,
unable to decide whether to come down or not
into this dark, impure world.

At that moment
I heard a divine voice
from the summit of Aruṇācala:

"To the meadow flower looking with open eyes,
to the honey bee jumping from the flower,
to the skipping kid nibbling the grass,
to the reeling wind intoxicated with its fragrance,
to the myna darting with outstretched wings,
to the baby laughing with open arms,
to the dog running aimlessly,
to the lunatic laughing at the dog—

"Welcome on this brilliant morning!"

VIII

Everywhere
flowers blossomed
in this light.

"In this world
is there a single lotus of a heart
which has opened its petals to this light,
showering for aeons
in a downpour from the sky?"
asked the divine voice.

"O dwellers of this earth,
eternal travelers,
you who face a new life,

"Fill the cups of your hearts
with this divine nectar of light!"
the voice exhorted.

IX

The morning voice which resounded
through all corners of the earth
spoke from somewhere under the blood,
even in men absorbed in activity,
as the mysterious, unexpressed memories
of many lives . . . .

The meadow grass starred with flowers
at the shining edge of a forest
on the shores of an island
washed by the waves of the blue sea,
the pure song of a mountain stream,
the sacred bath on the banks of a river,
the clear, innocent, bright laughter
from the jubilant heart of a child,
the beautiful, half-remembered wandering in dreams,
the inexpressible joy emanating
from the depths of the heart—

Somewhere
in some folds of consciousness,
all this flashed
for a moment.
That is all!

Later—

The usual dark layers covering the mind:
annoying thoughts,
complicated dealings.

X

Hiraṇyagarbha[10] holds
the animate and inanimate world
in an effulgent, thousand-armed embrace;
yet not a single heart rejoices
in his spontaneous friendship.

The light in hearts
does not give luster to eyes.
The richness of life
is not echoed in a single voice.

With tortured looks which cannot bear
the immense splendor dancing all around,
people crawl
into the bonds of dark desires,
into the intricacies of superfluous thoughts,
into the obscurities of earning a living.

XI

Look!
Shadows are slowly
slithering under the rocks
like snakes;

the birds in the tree branches are chirping,
their feathers ruffled by the tickling
of the cold fingers of wind;

the cooing of doves
in the dark of the tree overhead
is drawing sleep over my eyes;

the shimmering light on the stream
from the summit of Aruṇācala
is playing
with your feet.

XII

To these people,
to these half-blind men,
always raising their eyelids
to open their eyes to light,

how many great men,
with hearts melting for this wretched world,
expounded so many religions,
explained so many paths of salvation,
taught so many ways of realization!

XIII

Prophet after prophet,
seer after seer,
incarnation following incarnation,
came into this mire,
exhorted,
sang,
recited Vedas
pleaded,
and spread the light!

XIV

For shaking them from their stupor,
for chastising them for their petty sensual lusts,
for trying to open their eyelids closed to light,
for condemning violence and prostitution,
for preaching unpracticeable righteousness and
    difficult demeaning morals,
for obstructing their power, self-importance, and rights,
for threatening them with death, hell, and the wrath of God,

they stoned and tortured these bearers of divine message,
crucified them,
drove them away with slander,
imprisoned them,
plucked out their eyes,
hushed their voices!

XV

"Sufferers, come;
we will comfort you.
Lowly ones, shrink not with oppression;
you are blessed.
You poor and gentle people, don't cry;
the kingdom of heaven is yours.
You who are blinded with pride,
you who are insane with violence,
you who are ruthless in ambition,
do not forget there is a God."

Where are the prophets who cried thus
with a thousand voices
on mountain tops, in thoroughfares,
      near forest hermitages—
these merciful men,
who gave their blood, their happiness, their lives,
who swam against power and time?

XVI

How many yogis,
bearing divine message on their lips,
nectar in their voices,
fire in their eyes,
the majesty of an ocean in their hearts,
have come down
one after another,
to redeem the lowly!

XVII

Śrī Kṛṣṇa, who played
eternal wisdom on his flute
as a world enchanting song;
the Buddha, who extinguished suffering
with a peaceful smile;
Jesus, who descended, promising
to atone men's sins with his own blood;
Mohammed, who cut off heads
to penetrate into men's hearts—

today
all these are mere names
in religions, quarrels, poems,
and self-aggrandizement!

XVIII

Gandhi, who, established in non-violence,
tried to banish hatred;
Ravi,[11] who tapped at the door
of impenetrable hearts
with his immortal songs;
Ramaṇa, the veritable Dakṣiṇāmūrti,[12]
who spread wisdom through silence—

today there is not a trace in the world
of their having come and gone.

XIX

All this land, every atom of it, has soaked
in the blood of those who sacrificed for an empire,
for patriotism, for religion, for truth, for
vengeance, for love . . .
has soaked and dried—

What did they give to the world?
What did they gain
by walking through suffering,
by becoming fuel to the fire?

XX

When I was young I too sought
swamis and yogis, scientists and scholars.

But wherever I went,
I soon found
those who claimed to know
did not know.
So I returned.

There were only those who talked,
but no one who could show.

XXI

"The world is real."
"The world is unreal."
"All this is matter."
"All this is energy."
"There is rebirth."
"There is no rebirth."
"Man is supreme, humanity everlasting."

Quibbling and preaching thus,
men pass away
without a trace!

XXII

"God exists." "God does not exist."
"We are omnipotent—
we shall create life, stop death."

As they spoke these words,
they vanished into death.
leaving their disciples
helpless.

XXIII

"We will make everyone happy.
We will remove suffering."

How many intellectuals,
while saying this,
gathered pleasures for themselves,
then, struggling, died,
unable to enjoy them!

XXIV

Why have we come?
How did we come?
Whence did we come?
Where will we go?
Indeed, how is it we exist?

How did we meet?
What is happiness, what is suffering?
What is righteousness?
Who will tell?

Do you know?
Do I know?
Does the one who says he knows, know?
How does he know?

XXV

Why cannot man be happy?
How has he become so irrevocably corrupt?
Why does he not realize?
Why is he incapable?
Is this all there is to life?
Whom shall I question?
Whom shall I defy?

XXVI

Man's untold torment,
meaningless dreams,
unrealizable hopes,
unapproachable ideals,
insatiable passion,
incessant quest–
Who can explain them?

XXVII

"'Close your nose and stop your ears."
"Observe silence."
"Shut your eyes."
"Hold your breath."
"Drop flowers on stones."
"Burn people of other faiths."
"Sit on a mountain top."
"Take a dip in a river."
"Stay in solitude."
"Make pilgrimages."
"Stop eating."
"Feed others."
"Leave the world."
"Gobble the world. . . . "

Thus, there is no end
to the books, preachings, scriptures, religions!

XXVIII

Listen to the restless gasping
of the wicked rogues
who hardened their hearts without mercy,
plundered the helpless,
made their own happiness their *summum bonum!*

Look at those struggling wretches,
stifled in the fat which they sedulously grew,
thinking they were nothing but the body and the senses!

XXIX

Afraid that some wise words
might unfinger their grip on the world
or open their eyes to light—
look, how they pass away
with downcast eyes and sidelong glances,
pretending innocence,
hiding from the sky
in their cringing bodies!

XXX

Nurturing their ego,
thinking there is no one wiser, stronger,
more capable than they,
blinded and fattened
with the arrogance of power—

Look!
The tiger of death
from within the depths of the cavern of time
is stalking these moose
whose iron hooves
trample the tender hearts
of the helpless!

XXXI

Trying to stop time
with their speed,
to smother the inner call
with their clamor,
to escape from their pettiness and helplessness
in the haste of work,
fearing that sometime, somewhere,
they might have to stand alone
before their souls—
Look
how they are trying
to dart through air!

XXXII

Imagining that whatever is lacking today
will be gained tomorrow,
abandoning this moment,
searching for that morrow which never comes—
who is to save these groping people
crying out for help?

XXXIII

Dearest, what a wonder is this world!

The light vanishing into the sideling clouds,
the smile slipping from your lips toward your cheek,
a flash one moment, forgetfulness the next.

Darkness,
endless darkness,
darkness into which
not a ray of light can peep!

XXXIV

Do not think of the jasmine
which fell on your bed last night.
That night is no more.
No memories, however great,
can sweeten your lips with passion.

Tomorrow?
How many tomorrows have become yesterdays?
Could our hopes and plans change a single tomorrow
to our liking?

XXXV

Even infinite time is only a moment.
In that momentary time, our life is but one moment.

Now, an awareness of you and I.
The next moment, neither you nor I.

That which is no more
will never come back.

XXXVI

In the infinite past
we were not;
in the infinite future
we will not be;
in the fathomless emptiness
without beginning and end,
just for a moment—
this flash called I!

XXXVII

Look
at these debased,
stubborn creatures
wailing!

See how despotic, cruel fate
thrusts them by the scruffs of their necks
into the dreadful, gory abyss
within the fangs of death!

The dew drops shining
on the blue flowers in the meadow,
the stars lighting the fathomless sky,
are being washed away
unable to resist.

These moments
of drawing your face toward mine
will never be found again,
even if we search
the whole universe.

XXXVIII

Form, beauty, hope, love, tears
are being swept away
in the swiftly running stream of time
to disappear in an ocean
of nothingness.

XXXIX

It breaks up empires, dynasties, ideals,
intertwined arms,
deep-rooted dogmas,
plucks and pulls
by roots.

XL

Neither prayer nor tears,
censure nor praise,
appeals nor offerings
can stop
the hobnailed march of Fate.

XLI

Relentless Fate
watches foolish hearts
building loves,
hoping for immortality—
What a joke for Time!

Is there no comfort
for this blood-retching
pain and suffering?

XLII

Do you hear
the last wails
of beings who,
under illusion
there is something somewhere,
crawl with broken backs and dragging feet
into the venomous, cavernous mouth
of the terrible serpent
of death?

XLIII

Is there a Lord
who cares for the abandoned
raising their arms in helplessness?
Is this all a meaningless,
futile lamentation?

XLIV

Is it not better
not to be,
than to be
and be
useless,
helpless,
and hard-hearted?

XLV

My love!
Even if taking life is acceptable,
killing love is unpardonable.

If there be a terrible god who destroys love,
could the world ever forget its suffering
and forgive him?

XLVI

Singing hymns before Viṣṇu,[13]
incessant meditation on Kailāsa,[14]
delighting in logic in the presence of Brahmā,[15]
dancing with Apsaras[16] in heavenly regions,
meeting with loved ones in the presence of Allah,
a high seat beside Jehovah—

Desires!
Endless petty desires,
self-deceptive belief,
sky-devouring, cunning selfishness!

"Give to me,
not to him.
Give here,
not there—"
such are man's desires!

XLVII

"God's will!
Cruelty, fear, death, torment—
it's all God's will!"

"For us happiness,
misery for others.
Anonymity for others,
for us fame."

The scoundrels who say
it's all God's will—
as if they were guardians of God's
    secret consultation-chambers!

XLVIII

"It's all Karma!
My Karma is good!
Yours bad!

"You did it!
Now suffer the consequences!
Indeed, having done, you ask questions?!
Shut up!"

XLIX

If you have done something,
wherever and however you hide,
it will pursue and torment you.

Once you are caught in the clutches of Karma
there is no rescue,
no hope,
no release.

Falling over
and over
into the whirlpool,
floating a moment,
sinking to bottom the next,
    crying out in vain with hope,
arms raised toward the sky
struggling endlessly,
with suffocating torment—
no help.

That's all
there is
to life!

L

No way out, no hope,
no pity which comforts,
no way to escape
this
demonic, inevitable, dark cycle
of birth and death.

LI

With no way out
men bear forever
this cruel, merciless tyranny,
arbitrary and invisible.

Tasting a drop of honey
offered on the edge of a knife,
men suck the blood
oozing from the wound
and say, "What a boon!"

LII

Go on pilgrimages,
serve gurus,
study scriptures and Vedas,
look inside,
look outside—

how can the great mystery
of beginningless and endless creation
be known to the mind
which flashes and is extinguished
in one moment
somewhere
in the infinite flux of time!

LIII

Whom shall I ask?
Who knows?

If a creator exists,
let me see him!
I will stop and defy him!
I will ask, "What is all this about?"

But if the creator asks,
"Whom do you question,
who promised to make you happy
and clear your doubts?
Indeed, who are you
to ask me?
You,
your life,
your intelligence—
what are they?"
what shall I say?

LIV

It is all an unknown,
unknowable,
inexplicable,
profound mystery.

It is unwise to go round
in a circle leading nowhere
for some unknown,
chasing mirages
which delude us into thinking
there is something which,
if we strive for it,
will be revealed.

It's a futile waste
of an invaluable lifetime.

LV

Consider!
Who is 'I' who speaks to you?
Who is 'you' who listens?

Who are the others
between and who separate us?
Who is the light
which looks through these eyes
at you and me together?

Who is the listener
that takes in my words?
Who is the awareness
which stands behind,
deluding us into thinking,
"'I' am experiencing?"

LVI

Tired,
leaning your head against my chest,
sleeping—for you where is the world?
Where are the stars?
Where am 'I'?
Where are 'you'?

In the darkness
far from my gaze
behind your closed eyes,
where are 'you'?

Your mind wakes,
hearing me softly calling you 'dearest',
gives not a bit of news of that world.
What became of it
during that time?

LVII

Settled down, eyes closing,
our heads so close,
lain to sleep in union,
between your thoughts
and mine
how many oceans
of unbridgeable
gulf!

LVIII

When great passion,
single-minded and breath-stopping,
steps over the limits built by the mind
and merges in peace,

in that moment
you are not and I am not,
there is no difference of you and me:
the world ceases to exist.

LIX

When time moved out
from the womb of infinity,
a wave of awareness
spilled and leaped
on some shore of illusion,
and shone on the sky
as a spray of light.

LX

All this is one awareness!

The same dawn
which peeped hesitantly,
wondering whether she would be admitted,
reluctant to leave,
draws back one finger-ray after another
and disappears in the West.

The fierce sunrays
cruelly breaking with great passion
on the earth
tickle the midnight sky
with tiny, little lightning-kisses.

LXI

Did the *kastūri*[17] flowers' fragrance
show the blind *gurivenda*[18] vine
the way to the bough of a tree?

Did the *taṅgeḍu*[19] bush ever know
the chest measurements of the bee
drinking honey within its flowers' wombs?

Who taught the coconut tree,
dancing with open arms in the midday sun,
to weave fibre shirts to protect its child
from breaking loose and dropping
from its height?

Did the pregnant mother dream
where each limb of the baby in her womb
should grow?

Is it the fish
that changed the principle of creation
so that ice in the frozen ocean
would not become heavy?

LXII

Drinking the fierce sun's intolerable light,
the sky, perspiring like stars;
swallowing the mind of the yogi,
the cosmos of the heart, dancing with ecstasy;
adorning its head with firefly flowers of light,
the tree, yearning for beauty;
the endurance of the mother giving form in her womb
to the lover of her heart;
the ocean, longing to unite the earth with the sky
    and laugh—
all this is one awareness, one light,
dancing
with irrepressible excitement!

LXIII

The burning lake,
turned a hearth of flashing fire
by the searing rays of the sun,
pacified like the fury of Viśwāmitra,[20]
dreams of cloud-shadows
in the silence of the blue sky.

The shadows move,
the sunshine becomes hotter,
the faded flowers of night
with hanging heads keep time
to the dance of the new morning flowers.

LXIV

Sporting with diversity
the Sun God,
splendid with myriad colored reflections
in the scattered dew drops on the leaves of grass,
becoming fierce,
withdraws his multifarious forms.

The delicate earth's surface,
showered by the brilliance of the morning sun,
thrilled by its touch,
turns into the green meadow—
then unable to bear its intensity,
faints.

LXV

The passion of universal consciousness
knows no tears.

The eye of mercy which gave futile speed
to the deer trembling
at the roar of the bloodthirsty tiger
does not become damp.

The love which affectionately painted colors
on the wings of sunbirds
faints at the touch of the eagle's beak
tearing open its prey.

Not a single tear falls from the heavens
to console the heart of the mother
writhing at the helpless cry
of her baby seized by death.

LXVI

The goddess of woods,
wakeful all night,
decorating every blade of grass
with colored lights,

at dawn,
with infinite detachment
hands her decorations over
to the sharp, cruel tongue of the cow.

LXVII

There is no place for mercy
in the heart of creation's passion
breaking out in joyful abundance.

There is no count
of how many lives and how many loves
are destroyed day to day,
moment to moment,
by the stamping feet
of the dance of dissolution.

In this temple of Kāḷī—
every minute,
a great offering of a million lives.

The longing of separated lovers,
the agony of a mother in labor,
the attachment of a suckling baby,
the panicking despair of living beings approaching death—
all are sporadic postures
in her great dance
of cosmic gaiety.

LXVIII

How can I believe
mercy and love
rule the universe?

Divine light,
bright as myriads of suns,
could it not illumine
the darkness of petty human egos?

Must narrow, stupid whales roam about
in the infinitely wide and clear
ocean of consciousness
fattened by the flesh
of dainty, helpless fish?

Must the unceasing waves of love,
surging with everlasting attraction,
strike in vain for aeons
on hard, rough, stony hearts,
to be broken, spilled, and drained
as tears?

LXIX

In a heartless world
this life of servitude is unbearable.

We do not know what all this is for,
why we are born,
how we have fallen into this maze—
but there is no release.

Must we struggle on and on, for aeons,
being born again and again,
with interminable hopes and gnawing desires,
with ever-clinging pettiness?

Death?! What can it do?
How can death help,
death which can only burn a tired body
but not a burning mind?

LXX

"Is there not a savior,
a bestower of wisdom,
a merciful being to hold my outstretched hand?"—
Crying thus,
I closed my eyes.

"Dwell in my eyes;
be pacified in my speech;
rest in my heart;
conquer death in my love,"—

Thinking thus,
I slept in your arms
which do not let me go,
even in sleep.

LXXI

That same night I had a dream:

Red forms were rising
from brilliant white flames,
like *ghee* falling into sacrificial fire,
like twigs of firewood
flashing for a moment and becoming white,
mingled with the flames.

Empires, revolts, aeons, doomsdays,
leaping up like sparks
and shooting a little way,
joined as ashes
in the white flame of that sacrificial fire!

LXXII

"I! I!
What was I? Where?
Was I not in the flame
of that universal sacrificial fire?"
As I was thinking thus—

I was there!
And you?
You too were there;
I,
holding your finger,
in the bondage of mutual attachment:
we were standing
a moment,
pleading with time.

The next moment—
we fell inevitably into the flames,
our attachments and bodily bonds
burning away:
we became one
and disappeared!

LXXIII

When I opened my eyes
the first memory was
I!
Memories one after another
crawled around that 'I'
stinging like wasps!

The mind began its work!

Rising like deep, dark clouds from the East
on a clear autumn sky,
the black smoke of the earth
enveloped me and gave me shape—
I couldn't breathe.

The dream
was passing away,
receding.
Along with the dream
receded bliss.

Remained. . .
the heavy,
stifling
'I'.

LXXIV

Like Nalakūbara[21] who fell into mire
by some cruel curse,
with sorrow-stricken bewilderment
I looked at this world,
at you sleeping
your cheek resting on my hand!

Suddenly, an irrepressible wail
started from within me:
"Have I gotten entangled again,
dragging myself
into this maze of mind's attraction?"

Having sported all night,
as if all the worlds were our own,
immersed in joy,
have we awakened again
in this room,
in this body,
on this bed?

LXXV

Lord!
Is life just this,
only this for ever?

Won't you hear me?
Can't you hear me?
Even if you heard, can't you understand?
Is it impossible for you . . .?
Is there really nothing at all?

I can't bear it!
I can't stand it!

LXXVI

Trying to get up from the bed,
trying to free myself from your arms,
I looked at you
sleeping happily,
without a worry,
trusting that I was there to lean on,
to show the way, to save you.

"What can this unfortunate one give,
this accursed fellow,
this weakling
caught in the jaws of existence?"
I shrank with shame.

My infatuation for you,
your dependence on me,
my helplessness,
the strong bond between us—

Unless this is broken,
there is no release for me
nor salvation for you:
I am leaving!

LXXVII

As I was stirring to get up,
your fingers tightened
on my shoulder
like the roots of a storm-blown tree
twisting around a rock.

Your sleeping mind,
expecting me to lean over you,
smiled gently on your lips!
The jasmine in your hair
implored me with its fragrance
not to go!

LXXVIII

"Why do you so struggle?
What higher heavens are you going to attain
than the good fortune of embracing your woman?
What spiritual union will give
such an experience of bliss
as the drinking of honey,
perfumed with the quivering smile
on her red-petal, smooth lips?

"What gods will take pity on a fool
who tortures a loving heart,
endeavoring
to leave that which he has,
imagining that something he has not
will be found?"

LXXIX

"Are you a Buddha?[22]

Maybe you are only a Nala!"[23]

LXXX

Whatever it be,
I cannot bear this fire!

For me there is no more peace.
No longer is there sleep for me
on those breasts
which arrest my eyes
and undermine my resolve.

Woman,
let me go!

LXXXI

A call!

From Aruṇācala,
an irresistible invitation!

Without looking back,
I ran!

LXXXII

I ran
not knowing where I was going.

I ran
up the mountain into the dark.

Rocks rolling down,
trees grazing past,
thorns tearing flesh,
snakes giving way.

In front of me an infinite abyss—
I stopped.

LXXXIII

Aruṇācala—
granite wave of bliss—
light in the midst of darkness—

You who quell the suffering of becoming
    with a sidelong look,
You whose beacon of light
    burns away the bonds of all impurities,
You with soft, white, gliding clouds
    as cloak—

Śiva,
be gracious to me!

LXXXIV

Before me,
a shadow of light reaching the sky,
a dark form giving lustre
to the blackness,

A voice,
majestic and kind,
asking, "Who are you?"

LXXXV

"I. . . ."

"True. But who is that I?"

"I? I."

My gaze turned inward.

"Who is it that says 'I'?"

Yes. Who is it that says 'I'?

LXXXVI

Indeed, Bhagavān,[24]
who am I?
Who is this I?

Who shall I say is this I?
Who is this I that spun
a separate cocoon around itself,
saying "I"?

Separated
  from the light dancing over the whole universe,
  from the endless pulsations of life
    breaking into waves of births and deaths,
  from the experience of the human heart
    swinging between happiness and misery,
  from the expanse of the limitless sky
    fluttering its wings in order to be released,

Who is this I?
Indeed, who is it that says "I"?

LXXXVII

Who was I before creation?
Who is it that remains after creation?
Who is this consciousness,
witnessing steadily at all times, in all states,
unruffled and unchanging?

Who is the light
reflected, without being dissolved,
in the tears of happiness and misery?

Who is it that says "I"?
Who is it that knows
that there is this I?

Who? Who? Who?

LXXXVIII

That majestic dark form touching the sky
fixed its gaze on me,
like the flame of an intense fire piercing iron,
like a concentrated sun ray melting stones.

That glance, full of light,
entered into my darkness, like Brahmā's missile,
leaping into my innermost heart,
cutting all bonds,
burning in a blaze!

I was not!

LXXXIX

There was no I
nor whatever I was imagining as I;
a void within me,
a void filled with bliss;
outside of me
a void filled with light;
inside, outside—
everywhere—
Void!

XC

When I opened my eyes:
you, the room, sunshine
and I looking at them.

Lord!
have you let go
of my hand!

Again,
have I fallen
into this illusion!

XCI

"Don't cry!
All this matters not,
a dream without substance.
Who does the dreaming?"

As soon as I heard this from deep within my heart—

there was neither you, nor the room,
nor I, nor the world:
everywhere waves of bliss
saying, "I", "I".

XCII

The timeless, spaceless picture
I painted within myself:
you, I, the room, sunshine,
the sky, beauty—everything
is the cosmic consciousness within me:
I am everywhere.

The light in my heart,
refracted into colors
in the prism of the mind,
spilled and became the world.

XCIII

So it was,
until dawn kissed the still-sleeping darkness
    to open its eyes,
until the first sun-rays flashing on your fingernails
    shone on the walls,
until the breeze swinging on your breast
    sighed and reluctantly peeped out into the world,
until your outstretched hand
    searched for me on the bed.

So I sat,
forgetting myself
in the spontaneous, indefinable bliss!

XCIV

As honey
    loses itself in its own sweetness,
as the sky
    faints in its own blueness,
as fire
    shines in its own flame,
as light
    drinks its own brightness—

Bliss!
I who am I
have been tasting endless bliss
for so long!

XCV

Woman,
such is this world!

Glittering forms without reality
illumined by the light of consciousness
on the loom of space and time—
this is just a shadow puppet show!

Karṇa and Arjuna[25] who fought so long on the screen
lie down embracing
in the coffin of time.

Until the waves of the mind,
raised by the wind of desire,
subside,
the cosmic consciousness,
glowing with pure light,
will not be reflected
on the ocean of the mind.

Woman,
open
your
mind's
eye!

XCVI

That spontaneous cosmic play,
bound by form, taste, and smell,
finds fulfillment
in you, me, and everyone
as shades of happiness and sorrow.

XCVII

This fervor of life,
rousing itself from itself,
and breaking with its own force
into countless white dew drops of bliss,
is vibrating endlessly,
exclaiming "I, I."

With infinite variety of forms and names
it is dancing with joy
bound by the rhythm of life and death.

XCVIII

Love, beauty, and happiness
coupled with the essence of joy—
this world:
a picture you draw on your mind!

A victim of desire,
not knowing contentment,
you try to rectify
that picture,
changing it
from moment to moment!

Creating space and time,
your mind
weaves this illusion.

XCIX

Dearest, listen!
Just one principle,
just one way,
just one step to salvation!

If you watch
with a mind free of thoughts
the magic of Aruṇācala
moving before your eyes,
the stream does not flow on the mountain,
the wind does not blow in the trees,
the reeds do not sway in the water,
the clouds stand still in the sky,
the flowers remain unfading.

If you take the next moment
into your mind,
that moment
jealously
hides its nectar away
beyond your reach!

C

In this very moment,
in this bliss,
stay and be still.
Arrest time in your mind
so it does not move.

If the fingers of Anura[26]
stood without trembling on tightened reins,
the wheels of the sun's chariot
would stand unmoving.

Lasso your breath,
tighten the throat of your mind!

CI

If not,
stay in love,
love that makes you forget the world,
the body and passion.

Love!

Love withdraws your mind from your eyes
and stands in the silence
of the cavern of your heart—
remain in that love
from moment to moment!

Be arrested in my gaze
and stop your gaze.
If your eyes move,
your mind will move.
If your mind moves,
whole worlds move!

CII

I am your joy,
you are my delight,
all this is bliss.
Only this division
of you and me—
an illusion!

If you raise your eyes—
the endless sky with unreachable limits.
If you turn your gaze inward—
the unfathomable heavens of consciousness.

Don't delude yourself—
you are not just a body of four cubits length.

CIII

Shadows moving on the luminous screen of consciousness,
you, I, others
are all colors without substance.

There is no knower without the mind.
If there is no knower,
there is no you.
If you are not, then who is there for you?

Before you existed,
did the world concern you?
After you are gone,
will the world worry
what became of you?

The world is no mystery;
all illusion is of the mind!

CIV

No mind—
there is no you.
No you—
no world.
No world—
no suffering.
Then who is yearning
and for whom?

Differences, sorrows, diseases, and lamentations
are shadows of mind
hidden in "mine"ness
beyond the reach of universal light.

CV

You are not separate from
the knower and the known;
the joy and its experience—
you are both.

If you raise the curtain of mind
the bride and the bridegroom,
the lover and the beloved
become united
in one love!

CVI

All this is nothing but mere light.
It is not even that.
Although there is everything,
there is nothing—
nothing in which there is everything.

It is not what we imagine,
nor can imagine,
not anything,
nor nothing either.
Indeed there is not anything to be imagined—
there is nothing.

What it is—
know that
by stopping your mind!

CVII

If this mind is burnt,
there is no mind to know,
no need to know,
nothing to know.

The knowing mind,
the world known,
revealing God—
all are one!

One silence,
soundlessness beyond sound,
void which fills
everything!

CVIII

This fundamental principle,
Skanda,[27] the image of wisdom,
taught his father
on Mount Kailāsa.

This mysterious truth,
Śrī Dakṣiṇāmūrti,[28]
seated under a banyan tree,
made knowable
to the *siddhas*[29] who begged him.

With this same secret of Vedānta,
Śrī Ramaṇa Bhagavān,[30]
through voice, glance and silence,
opened the eye of wisdom
to the afflicted who sought his refuge.

References
(Introduction)

1. Gudipati Venkatachalam, *Chalam* (Autobiography) (Ramanasthan, Tiruvannamalai, 1973), p. 212.
2. As quoted in *Andhra Jyoti Daily* (Vijayawada, May 6, 1979).
3. From *Strī*, as quoted in Gorrepati Venkata Subbayya, *Chalam* (Biography) (Desi Kavita Mandali, Vijayawada, 1958), p. 288.
4. From a letter to Chinna Rao (April 10, 1952), as quoted in Subbayya, *Chalam*, pp. 248-249.
5. From *Kavigā Chalam*, as quoted in Subbayya, *Chalam*, p. 141.
6. *Prēma Lēkhalu* (*Love Letters*) (Yuva Book Depot, Vijayawada, 1944), Part 2, pp. 48-49.
7. From a review of *Citrāṅgi*, a play by Chalam, as quoted in Subbayya, *Chalam*, p. 250.
8. From an interview in *Andhra Prabha Daily* (Vijayawada, May 7, 1979).
9. From *Musings*, as quoted in Subbayya, *Chalam*, pp. 131-133.
10. As quoted in Subbayya, *Chalam*, pp. 288-289.
11. As quoted in Subbayya, *Chalam*, p. 257.
12. As quoted in Subbayya, *Chalam*, p. 259.

Notes to Poems

1. The Eastern part of the mountain Aruṇācala is regarded as Śiva, and the Western side, his wife Pārvatī. The goddess is worshipped with vermilion (*kumkum*), a red powder.
2. The moon.
3. A sign of begging.
4. A white flower used for decorating hair.
5. The Poplar-leaved Fig tree.
6. The moon.
7. The name of the constellation Tauri; also, the moon's wife.
8. Alexandrian Laurel.
9. Thorn apple.
10. Literally, 'One who is born of a golden egg;' that is, Brahmā, the creator of the universe.
11. Rabindranath Tagore, the Indian Nobel-laureate poet.
12. Ramana Maharshi is considered to be an incarnation of Daskṣiṇāmūrti, an aspect of Śiva without Pārvatī.
13. The central god in Hindu mythology: the sustainer of the universe.
14. The abode of Śiva, Mount Kailāsa.
15. The creator god who recited the Vedas at the beginning of creation. A symbol of scholarly and intellectual pursuits.
16. Celestial dancers.
17. The Babul tree.
18. Indian Shot (Wild liquorice tree).
19. The Tanner's Cassia.
20. A sage of ancient times known for his anger.
21. An angel who, for his mischief, was cursed to be born on the earth.
22. The Buddha left his wife and renounced the world to find enlightenment.
23. Nala, banished from his kingdom and unable to bear seeing his wife suffer, abandoned her in a forest. Later he remarried her and was again king.
24. A form of addressing Śrī Ramana Maharshi.
25. Halfbrothers who fought on opposite sides in the battle of Kurukṣētra depicted in the epic *Mahābhārata*.

26. The charioteer of the sun.
27. The son of Śiva.
28. Śiva without Pārvatī, his wife.
29. Bodiless spiritual beings.
30. Sri Ramana Maharshi.

The Translation

Narayana Moorty prepared the initial working draft of the translation. Sowris and Julie Wellings revised this draft. They read their version to Chalam and received his approval. Elliot Roberts, with the help of Narayana Moorty, polished the diction, phrasing and poetic form of the translation.

In this translation, the editors strove, as much as possible, for literal accuracy. However, because of the syntactical differences between the Indian languages—Sanskrit and Telugu—and English, the phrasing and sentence structure are different. More important, the stylistic uniqueness of *Sudha* could not be reproduced. *Sudha* has a heavy, powerful quality, a result of Chalam's unique blend of Sanskrit and Telugu. About 90% of the words are Sanskrit. A typical poem starts with a series of highly Sanskritic compound words and abruptly drops down toward the end of the poem into a few, light Telugu words, giving a sense of relief from the heaviness of the poem. This quality of the poem could not be conveyed in the English translation.

All quotations in the Introduction from the works of Chalam and other Indian writers have been translated from the original Telugu by Narayana Moorty.

The dedication to Iśwara is a carry over from the Telugu original.

The Translators

Narayana Moorty has an M.A. in Philosophy from India and a Ph.D. from the University of California, Berkeley. He has had experience in translating philosophical literature from English to Telugu. As an Assistant Compiler to the Philosophy and Religion volume of the Telugu Encyclopaedia he translated several articles which were published in it. Some of his other translations and original contributions appeared in reputable Telugu newspapers and magazines. He has also been published in Indian philosophical journals in English. He has taught both Eastern and Western Philosophy for a number of years in India and in the U.S. and is currently teaching at Monterey Peninsula College.

Sowris is a daughter of Chalam and is a mystic. She is a writer in her own right, having published several novels and biographies. She is well-versed in the nuances of Chalam's thought, having initially been educated through Chalam's works.

Julie Wellings is American and is a disciple of Sowris. She lived with the Chalam family in Tiruvannamalai.

Elliot Roberts has an A.B. from Columbia College and an M.A. in English from Cornell University. He is an instructor in English at Monterey Peninsula College, where he has taught world literature, poetry and creative writing. For many years, he acted as Coordinator of the College's Spring Poetry Readings. He is co-editor of a college textbook (*Bridges,* Prentice-Hall) and has one published volume of verse, *To Mary After Eight* (Peter's Gate Press, Monterey, 1973). His poems have appeared in *The Brand New Testament, Cannery Row 1971, Bridges,* and *The Rhetoric of Yes.*